POETIC MUSINGS

Reminisces
And
Random Thoughts

My life and work in poetic form

By

George Lark Ellison

A Passionately Fair Publisher

Publishing, Manuscript formatting, Cover designing
and interior artwork to portray
By
Pat Simpson
Director of the Writers & Poetry Alliance
www.apfpublisher.com

ISBN 978-1-4466-1993-3

Foreword

Dear Reader

It is with great pleasure that I present this body of work amassed over the last 17 years; I hope you enjoy the reading of them as I have in writing them!

These poems cover a wide variety of moods, sentiments, likes and dislikes and many different styles, which I have attempted to master Including two of my own invented styles **Take a Letter** in which each line begins with the nominated letter and the last line of verse being just one word and the **5's and 3's style,** which has 15, lines with a syllable count of: **5 –3 -10 -12–15 –18 –25 –30 -25 –18 –15– 12– 10– 3– 5**

I also have a created style called **George's Hourglass** This style has Twelve lines, Rhymed or unrhymed With syllables on each line as follows... **7,6,5,4,3,2,2,3,4,5,6.7**

I have started my book with poems **Poetic Musings done in my own created style** followed by **Verse** which best describes my thoughts on my own work, though the first poem I wrote was **Concrete Jungle.** A few of the poems are of my thoughts on the society in which I live and some of the subjects that really get under my skin!

Some of my poems are Humorous, well if we didn't have any fun, life would be pretty miserable for all of us, I have poked fun at people I know as well as myself, anyone who recognises themselves in any of my work please be assured it is all tongue in cheek

Some poems are of a romantic nature, there is always romance in all walks of life and I have taken a few liberties in the writing of some of these poems about friend's acquaintances and lost loves!

Then there are the best of the rest of my poems written in the last 17 years including **Fateful Forecast** a poem about the perils of the sea, **Lest we Forget** which was some years in the making as the event happened in 1973 and has been imprinted on my psyche ever since,

The Hug which was inspired by reading **Staying Alive** a compilation of poems from Bloodaxe Publishers who had two different poems of the same title and different lengths and I just thought I could do one on that subject hence the poem. **Brother Masons Harmony.**

This is a Masonic poem about performing after dinner to those present, it could just as easily fit any performing situation **Sir Bobby** is about Sir Bobby Robson and all he represented.
I hope you enjoy the rest without preamble as I say in

My Copyright some are better than others I know that without being told, but I put them into print so you can judge for yourself!

George L. Ellison

Contents

Contents

Contents

Contents

Contents

Now come along
take a walk with me
and as your eyes do
the walking

I hope you enjoy
all the muses you see,
and hopefully relate
in some way
to the Reminisces
and thoughts that
so randomly pass
through my mind

Poetic Musings
Take a Letter "P"

Pens and
Pencils, tools of our trade
Paper used a
Plenty

Probing thoughts
Peering around
Partial to certain subjects
Picky

Poetry comes in many forms
Prose is just one style
Perfecting text till it's just right
Precise

Performing ones own written work
Pitching to the crowd
Pacing about during the act
Playful

Polishing the final draft
Publishers are waiting
Printers ready for the text
Primed

Publicity next, that's the tricky bit
Personal choices vary
Perusal at the bookstore shelf
Payment?

Practice of verse and of rhyme
Pulls in every direction
Placing syllables in strict lines
Painful

Parting with one's innermost thoughts
Psychologically soothing
Primal desires stir the soul
Perfection?

Verse

Poetry, whose rhyming words
    Of moods happy and sad
They make the world a wonderful place
    When they make the heart be glad
They also can be nonsense
    When the words off times appear
To be laid down backside foremost
    When in the style of Lear
The daffodils, the jumblies
    The elegies and odes
I love them all and that's no lie
    As my style it begins to flow
With each new poem it's easier
    At least for now that's true
As I draw my inspiration
    From subjects old and new

I draw with words, my visions
       Of life just as I see it
I try to call a spade, a spade
       As my thoughts are illuminated
I know my poems they vary
       From good to just plain poor
The odd one may be better
       But that's for others to know
Me, well I just write them
       Sometimes just of the cuff
But I'd like to think the work I do
       Will be seen as good enough
I may not be a Wordsworth
       A Shelley, or a Keats
But they all started the same way
       So who knows what fate waits?

My Story

So you want to know my story
There isn't much to tell
I was born in the month of August
Under Leos' spell
Twas the year of the Dragon
As it will be in 2012
When I will attain sixty years
But on that let us not dwell
I only live ten miles
From the place where I was born
In a hospital in Newcastle
That is closed now as its tired and worn

At age four I was heard to sing
I would be seen on regular occasions
Often doing my thing
I was called "The Happy Wanderer"
From the tune I had on my lips
I never knew about the charts
But that tune just seemed to stick

I started school at Easter
They did that when I was young
But I was always a sickly child
So it wasn't that much fun

Then at fifteen there came a bombshell
That's why I have no kids
Hereditary is an awful word
If Pandora lifts her lid
As a result I do not drive

Because of my condition
I know others do who are so much worse
But that is my position

At twenty-one I went abroad
Europe for to see
But it was my time at Dachau
That made the biggest impression on me

In Seventy- four I made the trip
To the palace to be presented
To the Duke of Edinburgh
In the ballroom
Which was splendid
To receive my D of E award
For all the work that I did

I spent a few years hostelling
Where I met my ex and my best man
Then in eighty-two I met Sheila
And soon became a married man

The years since have had their moments
As always is the case
Some hopes fulfilled some shattered
Rarely being in the right place
But I always have my fallbacks
Like my music and my books
Not forgetting all of my poetry
All those topics, where to look
Styles they are a plenty
One day I'll have the time
To keep up with the others
But for now I'll write the odd rhyme

So now you have my story
Of mixed fortunes as you can see
But being a member of the alliance
In writing, is the making of me!

The Bookworm

Once upon a time
Were the first words that I read?
When first I started school
And in me there runs a thread
The love of books both old and new
Of authors many dead
Who have the gift of writing!
And of whom it's often said
They make the words do wondrous things
As they march across the pages
Who'd think that a simple alphabet
Could be so many themes and players
The characters they come alive
As places around them seem to thrive
When death can be an awful thing
But true love can survive

A romance or a thriller
Or a biography
A fantasy or chiller,
They all can enthral me
No matter what the mood is
Or if the day time grinds
It's nice at night to read a book
And leave the world behind
To lie in bed beneath the covers
Or to sit in an easy chair
You're never lonely with a book
And you never have to care
The hardest choice is what to read
The subjects are so varied
I'll try this one I've read before
As it's night and the book is scary
And when dawn comes and day begins
I'll start the new day over
I may even find a book so good
I'll read it from cover to cover

The Written Word

Putting pen to paper
     Is not as easy as it seems
Writing down on notepads
     What comes to you in dreams?
When writing about facts
     It's no good if it's fiction
The logic and the rhetoric
     The grammar and the diction
When writing about fiction
     You've got to know your facts
As the written word that you lay down
     Will be shown up for what they lack
So I'm off to library shelves
     To see what I can gather
To put my ideas of faction
     Without my critics being in a lather

The Wordsmith

I love to read
  I'd love to write
To compose with words
  And not be trite
To make the letters ebb and flow
  As story lines they come and go
As passages of finite text
  Make my readers wonder what comes next
To write a story
  Short or long
Or just write a poem
  That fills the heart with song
What ever I write I intend to enjoy
  The pleasure I get when words I employ
To gladden the hearts of all who come near
  This written work I hold so dear

Concrete Jungle

As I wander o'er the lonely fells,

And watch the sun shine down!

On all the multi-coloured hues,

Of green, gold, blue and brown.

I look beyond this beautiful scene,

To another not so bright!

What is it that scars my distant view?

An ugly building site!

When will it end I ask myself,

When will their funds run dry?

I cannot see an end in sight,

It makes a grown man cry!

They build and build and build and build,

Without a thought or care!

For the damage they cause and inflict!

On all the plants and wildlife that once resided there

The only thought they ever have,

Is for money, it's their god!

Much good may it ere' do them,

Should they live till one hundred and odd!

They'll live in a concrete jungle,

With no hills or dales or parks!

Bricks and roads will surround them,

It will look so very stark!

A legacy of mortar,

Is what we'll leave behind!

Unless a drastic change is made,

In the bureaucratic mind!

No more the walks along woodland paths,

In all kinds of weather!

No more the fields of corn and wheat,

No more the walks through heather!

No more the moss beneath my feet,

There'll be nowhere left to go!

The houses they'll not hem me in,

So it's off to sea I go!

Seasons

The leaves have turned a golden hue
 And also shades of brown
To me that augurs just one thing
 That autumn's come to town
Soon winter it will follow
 And autumn will take flight
As rain it turns to hail and snow
 And the frost begins to bite
Soon winter will increase its hold
 Till Santa's come and gone
And we herald in the New Year
 And the foggy early morn'
The March winds they will blow in
 And chase the fog away
The flowers they will start to bloom again
 As spring comes into play
The sap will rise up in the trees
 As once more they start to bud
And blossom will arrive once more
 As May strikes the right chord

And then comes June and summertime
And everyone feels great
The longest day has come and gone
Next come the months we hate
The clocks they now will soon go back
So too will the weather
As ticklish coughs become a hack
As winter it draws nearer
The cycle of life once more has turned
As seasons have come and gone
As winter once more takes a hold
We wait for the fresh spring dawn

The Stately Oak

What a wondrous sight to see
　　So many shaped woodland trees
As sunlight dances through the pines
　　It's time to leave the world behind
To lean against a mighty oak
　　And marvel at its splendour
As elm and ash both cut a dash
　　Another day will soon surrender

The chestnuts with their upturned flowers
  Of pure virgin white
Ivy clinging to sycamores
  And most every tree in sight
Rhododendrons spray the ground
  With multi-coloured petals
And new-formed trees begin their growth
  They're so fragile when they're little
As willows weep into the stream
  Through their vale of tears
As birch, and beech sway in the breeze
  The sun it disappears
But the tree that I love most of all
  Is the high and mighty oak?
Though everyone is much the same
  A lump comes to my throat
As all are individual
  Though very much alike
None can compare with the stately oak
  Who rules the woodland with all his might?

Reminiscence

The Pace of life can be so fast
> Tight schedules can make one gasp
So given the chance I let the pores exude
> The feeling of utter solitude
To take time out, let my thoughts just fly
> Allow the day to pass me by
To go at my pace just for once
> Ease my soul and let my thoughts bounce
Around my head they bob and weave
> As all around me I perceive
The rustling leaves the trickling stream
> The scented air and the sunlit scene
To look around the woodland glade
> As the trials of life are allowed to fade
To think of nought but what I see
> A falling leaf, a quivering tree
Many years ago it was all like this
> We had the time we were at peace
But all that changed with this new age
> As time sped up with each turning page
I yearn to be in yesterday
> It now seems oh so far away
When we all had time for everyone
> And looked forward to the rising sun
To set a pace we'd all enjoy
> Each man and woman, girl and boy
To love thy neighbour as thyself
> To lend a hand not keep to oneself
But the wheel of life rolls on and on
> As we all head for the setting sun
So I take my chances so I don't miss
> My times of solitude and bliss

My Woodland Hideaway

When first I found this little wood
    I knew it was the place I could
Open my mind let my thoughts run free
    Write my most inspired poetry
To be at one with mother earth
    To hear the stream, see springs rebirth
See blossoms bud on branch and stem
    At my hideaway from life's mayhem
To think of naught but verse and rhyme
    To enter my little world time after time
To smell the scented woodland air
    Be a contented poet without a care
If only this was always true
    Sometimes I'm oh so moody blue
Life on occasions gets me down
    I'll wander about with a frown
I look forward to my rest and play
    When I can enter my woodland hideaway

Little Border

His head it nods from side to side
Twinkling eyes are open wide
As up at you he'll sit and stare
Wondering what you've got there
His little beard, his bushy brows
A love within you is aroused
Like most dogs he can do no wrong
When he fills your heart with song
His wiry coat, his wagging tail
The holes he digs to no avail
He struts along without a care
As he's a Border terrier

Life of Riley

It was in the year of 84
When my Border Terriers
I first got to know
Sitting amongst the bales of hay
In Witton on a summers day
Home he came with my wife and I
Where a warm fire and radiators
He did espy
No more the outdoors
In the kennel for he
Truly had discovered the life of Riley
Many since have been and gone
But they all enjoy the heat bar none

The Good Life

Rolling waves break on the shore,
Lapping the sand and shingle once more,
I look out to sea, as a gull cries on high!
Then dives for a fish, in the blink of an eye
To feel as free as a bird on the wing,
It must feel good to soar and sing!
Yes you can fly, see as far as you care,
But there have to be drawbacks; up there in the air.
All beings have their limits,
As well as their gains,
So a seabird can fly,
But on land I'll remain!
I'll just have to paddle,
Instead of making a splash,
If I was meant to have wings,
I'd find them on my back!
We should all be contented,
With our lot in life,
Make the most of what's given,
It can save all the strife!
I'll walk along the seashore,
Look out to sea
I'll think that yes I've a good life,
I know so has he!

Mortality

How deep the roots
     How broad the trunk
How many rings to the tree
     It makes one think
To delve and burrow
     Like woodpeckers do
To research the living
     The long dead too
Generations are many
     But how many have I
Ancestors, Descendants
     Still around when I die
It can be less like a tree
     More like a weed
As one follows Mortality
     Through that old demon seed
To know where you came from
     Is important to some
To know where you're going
     Is important bar none

Those Were the Days

English rural country life
      Hear church bells toll
See birds take flight
      As I wander down the hedge-lined lane
Thinking of my youth again
      Hurrying to do my chores
Then playing conkers with the boy next door
      Staying out till fall of night
Do I have to come in?
      Yes, it's bath-time all right
Until tomorrow, I'll see you again
      All right, till then, I should go in
Those were the days
      When we'd run and hide
 Leave our doors open wide
      No one would rob you then
There was not much to steal
      Unlike today
When they'd take your bike wheel
      I still look at the old days
Through rose tinted glasses
      When the boys were the lads and
The girls were the lasses
      If only the circle could turn back again
But unlike our successors
      We can all but dream

The Workers Lament

I get up every morning
 A job of work to do
But how long will I keep it
 It's not up to you or me
It's up to higher management
 And sometimes they're not immune
From those at the very top!
 The ones who call the tune
Those faceless individuals
 Who never really care?
If any of us ever work
 For six months or a year
As long as the daily balance sheet
 Is weighed well in their favour
It's easy to forget the plebes
 Who get a pittance for their hard labour!
Still someone's got to do it
 It might as well be me
For if I were to be out of work
 A sorry sight I'd be
So let's not grumble, let's not groan
 Let's not cry or sob
But let's be happy in this last thought
 At least I've got a job!

Day of Rest

It feels good to be away from work

    With the tension left behind

So what, I've got to go again

    But today, let's just unwind

I'll wander through the woodland

    Or walk across the fell

To let my mind go walkabout

    Let my thoughts just dwell

To think of naught in particular

    To give the brain a rest

Away from pressures that day to day

    Can fill you full of stress

To lean against an oak tree trunk

    Gaze through branches to the sky

Watch as all the cumulous nimbus cloud

Wind driven passes by

To sit down in a peaceful spot

Just let yourself relax

Think why should I care a jot

As I gaze around under the noon-day sun

The only person who really counts

Is me, I'm number one

A number is all anyone of us is

When we see the setting sun

So I'm not going to care anymore

I'll do my job of work

As long as I can have days like these

I'll enjoy my time off taking my ease

Pollution

Water has a crystal gleam,
    When it begins its course as a mountain stream,
Clean and pure, it begins its fall,
    Down mountainsides steep and tall
As a stream it falls through hill and dale,
    Cutting a swathe down the length of its trail,
Full of life in many forms,
    See the angler wait with his tin of worms.
On it goes through leafy wood,
    Where native flowers come into bud,
Over falls, through weirs and eddies,
    Starting so pure, ending so muddy.
Past fallen trees and wrecks of cars,
    Past boxes, tins and empty jam jars,
The flotsam of life of is nowhere better mirrored,
    Than a walk beside streams as they turn into rivers.
The river meanders through village, town and city,
    Becoming more polluted, it's such a pity,
That man cannot clean up his act, but just blunder blindly on,
    Till the river isn't so much water, but more pollution.
The river becomes an estuary,
    As it wends it's way out to the sea,
The sea dilutes the toxic waste,
    But it's still in there for the sea-life to taste.
Eventually it breaks up,
    As it gets further out to sea,
Let's hope there's not an oil spill,
    As pollution is such a bitter pill!

Millennium Confusion

So you think it's the Millennium?

Well I've got some news for you

The next Millennium starts on

Two Thousand and One

You've jumped the gun my son

You're still in the Twentieth Century

The last of its years, that's true

Come Midnight on December Thirty-first

The Millennium will the be new

The Third one of its kind my dear

The bells will ring anew

But what of the year Two Thousand

It will be a part of the past

THAT'S TRUE!

Ode To The Mindless

Wheel treads scar the blades of grassy sod
        And leaves behind a sea of mud
A year it will take to repair the morass
        To overcome the deeds of the mindless
But as each year goes by it gets much worse
        While we pedestrians edge past and curse
At cars and vans parked on paths and grass
        Whilst the disabled cannot pass
Perhaps one day they will see the facts
        In blocking the way on grass and paths
Of their ignorant ways and selfish acts
        If they are disabled, disgruntled and cross
With no way around for them to pass
        They will see the circle turn in full
See once and for all how the mighty fall
        Now that they can plainly see
Through the eyes of their disability
        The moral here is plain to see
What goes around can come back for free
        If you wish to park wherever you like
Be prepared for the future to bite.

Recycled Thoughts

We take glass unless it's broken
        We take paper if it's not too wooden
We don't take card, as it's too hard
        Nor paper if it's glossy
We are not fussy,
        We are just choosy
We take tins by the hundred but
        We don't take plastic as that's too drastic
We like to think we give a service
        We like to think that we are green
Our customers may think we are a mess
        That our ideas are not what they seem
One thing is for sure
        We are all at sea
Our ideas of keeping our planet green
        Is way off the mark, we are not what we seem
Perhaps, if we recycled our thoughts
        Didn't just pretend
Our customers green ambitions
        Would be met halfway in the end
A greener planet could then be achieved
        If every last one of us could start and believe
That what was put out would be taken away
        Whether glass or plastic, tin or card
Magazines or papers it shouldn't be hard
        Virtually everything is recyclable
It just needs effort and the will applied
        Then generations to come could live longer lives

Language Barrier

I'm afraid it's been decided
By those up at the top
You must refrain the use of local slang
You really must talk posh

I could not believe it when I heard this
I've Taaked this way for years
If others cannot understand
They should do something with their ears

They say it is offensive
To call someone love or pet
Not to call a woman hinny
Is the daftest I've heard yet?

I don't mind being called Geordie
Bonny lad's okay with me
I've asked around this Geordie land
People think the council
Is out of its tree

The singsong tone of our dialect
Is not as hard to understand
Than other English regions
Who are really hard!

And yet

We are the one's who have to change,
I don't see why that should be
As beauty is in the ear of the beholder and
I sound all right to me

Spring Fever

Spring is here it's time to clean
      Time to get out mister sheen
Go berserk around the house
      From room to room with polish and clout
Scrape the paper bare the walls
      First the lounge then the hall
The kitchen ceilings' full of grime
      We'll do that next when we have the time
It's time to throw away last year
      What can we shed without a tear?
That can go so can they
      Something here has got to give way
Charity bags full to the brim
      Of things it's taken years to gain
Back to work and the smell of paint
      I only hope that I don't faint
Onwards and upwards the bedrooms are next
      So are the arguments we're getting vexed
Hard to get to nooks and crannies
      Don't you dare throw that out, it came from granny
The bedrooms are done
      The bathroom is gleaming
I can't wait for next year
      To do the spring cleaning

Sunday Supplement

A sunny Sunday afternoon
      Chilling out to a radio tune
Beethoven's' Sonata of the Moon
      Then it starts,
The lawnmower drone
      Like echoes
All around the square
      Someone joins in
It isn't fair
      All I want one day a week
Is to sit back and relax
      And
Not hear a peep
      Is it too much to ask?

To sit and slumber
        When I hear DIY
And the sound of a hammer
        Children crying fit to burst
I just don't know
        If it can get any worse
On it goes
        With a break for lunch
If they only had it as a bunch
        But no
They take turns
        To relieve us of noise
Someone is always
        Playing with their toys
Then finally
        At fall of night
Peace is restored
        Kids stop their fights
We breathe a huge sigh
        Of relief
As they go indoor
        For the working week

Night Shift Blues

Night shift to some
    A brief interlude
To some it's
    Permanent servitude
Rarely feeling
    The suns warm rays
Turning ever paler
    Gaunt and grey
To see daylight
    In all its' glory
And never feel
    The need to worry
About the twilight
    Evening hours
When work time beckons
    And darkness glowers
It can't be healthy
    To work when sleep
In your body clock
    Biorhythmic creeps
The natural order
    Of a symmetric soul
Is always required
    To make one whole
Some day it will end
    Someday I'll retire
I just hope in the meantime
    I don't expire
To live long in retirement
    Is my next goal in life?
To do what I want to
    And live a full life

Carbon Footprint

What can we do to save the planet?
And all life forms that move upon it
From buildings lit up like Christmas trees
To the standby left on our TVs
Around the corner
To schools in the car
Long haul flights
To countries afar
It's not easy I know
To go totally green
Reduce our carbon footprint
Become natures friend
But let's give it a go
Turn the drip off that tap
Switch off the light
Pat yourself on the back
Recycle refuse
Grow your own crop
You don't always have to
Drive to the shop
Fall in love with nature
She'll be your best friend
Beware global warning
This could be the end!

Votes For All

Why is there so much apathy?
　　　　When it comes to a vote
Don't you know it's for free?
　　　　There was a time
When votes were denied
　　　　To one and all nationwide
Till workers fought
　　　　For workers rights
So everyone could vote
　　　　Without a fight
The suffragettes got
　　　　Women the vote
At no small cost
　　　　To the lives they lost
So please remember
　　　　The dark days of the past
Have enshrined votes for all
　　　　When you next go to cast
You have freedom of choice
　　　　Vote for whom you like
So please cast you vote
　　　　Don't give up the fight
Even if you waste your vote
　　　　You're free to make that choice
So next time when it's polling day
　　　　Let them hear your voice
It didn't come cheaply
　　　　The say that you've got
So make your vote count
　　　　It matters a lot!

Paper

I'm a piece of paper
    Fresh from a block of wood
I'm destined for a paperback
    A thriller and it's good
I hope the reader who buys me
    Treats me with respect
Always using a bookmark
    As folding hurts like heck
I don't think that there is anything worse
    Than to be dog-eared folded and bent
So please, if you pick me up and buy me
    Treat me with respect
With care I'll last a lifetime
    You could read me more than once
Pass me around to family and friends
    Or to anyone you want
But one thing I'd ask before I go
    Please ask them to be aware
Treat me with the respect you've shown
    Make sure they treat me with care
I think I've said all I need to say
    Though I'll ask you to beware
Paper is a living thing
    We have feelings and we care
So be careful with us from now on
    We get fragile if we're torn
We'll help you burn the midnight oil and
    Chase your boredom in return!

Freedom For All

What is Freedom?
        Is it taken for granted?
In the western world
        Where Democracy's planted
If only that choice
        Was open to all
Freedom's destroyed
        When Democracy falls
We in the west
        Should count our blessings
If we lived further east
        We would learn a hard lesson
Freedom is
        But a pipedream to some
Forever under the heel
        Of the bomb and the gun
An eye for an eye
        In their Freedom fight
It's just one vicious circle
        As they meet might with might
Yes we can say as
        We look from a distance
Our land of the Free
        Was by birth our deliverance?
Free by birth
        In our own little bubble
But there are many less fortunate
        For whom life's a struggle
So we pray that one-day
        There'll be Freedom for all
With global peace
        When tyranny falls

Bollards

Standing like soldiers
    On central reservations
Of all major roads
    Throughout the nation
Like wizards hats
    They take their place
To become a blight
    On the human race
As traffic huddles
    In single file
Forming queues
    That stretch for miles
Cars ease forward
    At snails' pace
As drivers edge toward
    Workers in place
Relaying tarmac
    Cutting grass edges
Replacing lights
    Or just causing chaos
As they practice at nights
    Whatever the reason
There are no escaping bollards
    Whatever the season

On Reflection

When first we met
        I knew that I loved you
It seemed our relationship
        Would blossom in you too
We had our good times
        Our arguments also
Then after two years
        It was time to let go, so
We went our separate ways
        Not to hear from each other
Till many years later
        Both older and wiser
Our friendship rekindled
        Though only platonic
We're friends reunited
        And happier for it
On reflection perhaps
        We just weren't meant to be
But a distant acquaintance
        Is alright by me

A Question of Balance
(Fall Up)

What a silly thing to do,

    I've split my finger bone in two!

How long will it take to heal?

    As long as pain remains I feel!

Arthritis will be next it know,

    As bumps and bruises come and go!

The years weigh down my weary frame,

    As I stand up just to fall again!

You should fall up is a favourite cry,

    As one who knows me passes by!

I know they're right and I really try,

    But balance is hard when things go awry!

Perhaps next year I'll get it right,

    I'll keep my balance without a fight!

I'll walk, I'll work, and it will be plain to see,

    That I have conquered gravity!

Penny Wise

Look what I've got, come and see
When I bought two I got one free
On special offer just this week
Or while stocks last there will be more to seek
She'll nose around for a bargain buy
Scour the shops with her deadly eye
Missing nothing if it's cheap
If there is only one left to its rescue she'll leap
I've come home with one I wish I'd bought the other
What was I thinking as my nickname's special offer?
There are bargains galore in every store
This is all I can carry I'll go back for more
Another day she's back once more
Popping into shop and store
Looking for those bargain buys
Pennies make pounds for Penny Wise

Pound Foolish

I must go out to the shops again, to spend my weekly wages
I was on the Front Street yesterday, yet to me that seems just ages
A yearning fills my breast once more, to shop around and ponder
What has taken me all week to earn?
In the blink of an eye I'll squander
Like running water through my hands,
Money trickles through my fingers
I must get this, then I'll get that, Money is not allowed to linger
Soon once more I'll be spent up, nay look, now I'm insolvent
Perhaps this time my lesson's learnt, In the face of the lack of finance
I cannot resist a shopping spree; I must go and see a shrink
Be more controlled with money, and not buy before I think
Do I really need this; is it a price I can afford?
If not, walk on don't touch it, be strong say no find the door
Then much later and much shrewder, I'll buy only what I need
Then on special offer, I think I've taken heed
Pound-foolish am I no longer; I'm careful what I spend
I've been there got the tee shirt, now my ways I will amend
I've money in the bank once more; I've seen my savings grow
My debts are paid, I can breathe again,
and it's a pleasure not to owe
There's always the temptation, and sometimes I find it hard
Not to fall back into my old ways, so I've cut up my credit cards
I only spend now what I can afford, No matter what my hearts' desire
I hope the moral of this tale, Can other spendthrifts at some time inspire?

Alternative Phonetic Alphabet
(ABCDarien)

A is for Apple so tasty and sweet

B is for Botox to keep one so neat

C is for Cuddly so warm and secure

D is for Daddy so steady and sure

E is for echo, for echo, for echo

F is for Freddie who ever he is

G is for George brother of Freddie?

H is for Hope that I'm right all along

I is for Impetuous for those in love

J is for John related to above

K is for Kilo I got one right at last?

L is for lover that's not right, oh blast!

M is for Mike I think now that's three?

N is for Norman a bird found by me!

O is for Orange related to Apple

P is for Posy Brides throw at the Chapel

Q is for Queen HRH to you, me and others

R is for Romeo was he a lover

S is for Sugar sweet to take away bitter tang

T is for Tango a bright orange dance

U is for Umbria an Italian Province

V is for Vexed though I'm not annoyed

W is for whiskey that gives great joy?

X is for X-Ray a see through plate

Y is for yodel and the noise it makes

Z is for Zachary my good old mate

Always Believe
ABCDarien

Always **B**elieve **C**hrist's **D**eath **E**volved **F**or **G**od
Has **I**nstilled **J**oyful **K**indness **L**oving **M**entality **N**ow
Over **P**eople **Q**uerying **R**eligious **S**criptures **T**ill **U**nderstanding
Verifies **W**ith **X**trordinarily **Y**outhful **Z**eal

Book Critique

(Alphabetter)

A diluted book
All the best bits included
Any subject alluded
Abridged

Brightly coloured pictures
Bold text imprinted
Bindings made to last
Beautiful

Casts of many thousands
Could be only one or two
Come take me out on loan
Consider

Delightful storytelling
Delicate yet intense
Dedicate to a friend
Decide

Enjoyable page-turner
Exciting to the last
Elegant in all things
Exquisite

Finely executed
Filled with passion and despair
Fruity little segments dotted here and there
Fantastic

48

Gold embossed edges
Greatly enhanced by
Gifted Handiwork
Glorious

Heavy tome of many pages
Handed down stories from many ages
Holds the reader till the end
Haunting

Illuminating work
Ideas a plenty
Insightful manuscript
Imaginary

Joyous uproarious
Jolly good yarn
Justly nominated
Jubilant

Keeps up pace from first word to last
Kaleidoscope of characters
Knockabout comedy
Kookiness

Laugh a minute
Lung bustlingly funny
Lovely read
Lively

Magical moments
Moving to the point of tears
Must read
Magnificent

Number one bestseller
Nerve tingling
Non-stop pace
Nailed

Opulent surroundings
Overbearing parents
Oddball people
Outstanding

Precious caring moments
Perfect to a fault
Page-turner till dawn's early light
Precise

Quality writing from one of the best
Qualifies for major prize
Quantifies the reasons why
Quaint

Rip Roaring
Rib tickling
Rambunctiously funny
Rousing

Stunningly visual in every way
Such a well-rounded script
So much better than the previous book
Splendid

Tour de force
Terrifyingly authentic
Tremendously captivating
Tantalising

Unequalled by contemporaries
Unique in his/her field
Undeniably top of the tree
Unparalleled

Very good at what he/she does
Varies styles consistently well
Vividly scenic script
Valid

Well-worked characterisation
With a good plotline
Worth watching
Winner

Xeres never thought of that quote
Xylophones as props that's new
Xanadu as always the place to be
Xerox

Young children will love this book
You should open my pages and take a look
Yell from the rooftops how good I am
Youngster

Zealous with pen the story outline
Zestful witty and sublime
Zippy with a touch of calm
Zinger

*Alphabetter is the big brother to Take A Letter
The rules are the same but only one stanza is allowed per letter all 26
must be used

Accidental Damage

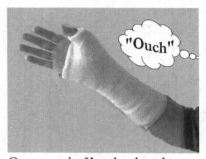

"Ouch"

Once again I've broken bones,
This time it is my wrist!
I'm wearing a pot to remind me,
Of the holiday I've missed!
My timing it was perfect,
After two weeks back at work,
I fell from a height with all of my weight and
Put my right hand in reverse!
Why am I so prone to accidents?
It always seems to happen to me,
The only thing I haven't done,
Is fall out of a tree!
I long to live a full year,
When accidents there are none,
Because forever going to A and E,
Just isn't that much fun!
The smell of disinfectant,
And looking at blank walls,

Is not how I want to spend my days?
Waiting for the doctor's call!
I've broken metatarsals,
And fingers more than one!
I fell off a gate and split my head,
Wide open when I was young!
I put a chisel into my hand,
I'm not good at DIY!
Once when screwing hinges,
The driver blade went in my eye!
I've always been a walking disaster!
If it's going to happen, it will happen to me!
I've cost the state a fortune,
And I'm only fifty-three!
So what else is around the corner?
What can possibly go wrong?
I'll have to wrap myself in cotton wool,
I won't stay young for very long!
Old age and infirmity,
Are curses we, all of us fear!
So it's time I looked out for myself,
As an accident could cost me dear!

Quiet

When everything is going well
And nothing seems to break the spell

DON'T MENTION THE Q WORD

When things are going at a pace
And the hands on the clock seem to race

DON'T MENTION THE Q WORD

When all around is hunky dory
And you dare to think of home time glory

DON'T MENTION THE Q WORD

There'll be time enough for a twist of fate
Without the mention of the word we hate
So if you don't want to get home late

DON'T MENTION THE Q WORD

The Hard Sell

I hear a knocking at the door
> So I pad across the floor
With dogs running at my heels
> First there are barks
Then there are squeals
> I open the door just a crack
As a man with a clipboard peers back
> Would you like double-glazing he coyly asks?
As he starts on his impossible task
> If you look around I think you'll find
I'm double-glazed at the front and behind
> Ah! Says he, now I see,
We do some nice conservatries
> We can fix your roof
We can pave your drive
> Our estimates are free
Won't you let me try?
> I'm afraid I won't
There's the Phone, goodbye
> I shut the door and go to the phone
Breathe a sigh of relief that he has gone
> Hello I say down the telephone line
Is that Mr.'X'can I prevail on your time?
> Before I can say no she is spinning her line
Would you like a new kitchen?
> We do some nice ones in pine

The 3 O'clock Shower

If rain is due
It will come at three
When the dogs start to bark
And I clip on their leads
At two forty-five
It's as dry as a bone
And it usually dries up
When I get back home
Is there a magic eye?
Up In the sky
Because when rain is forecast
I can never stay dry

Gadgets Galore

What did we do in the old days?
What did we do in times past?
Before we had our gadgets,
We had to make things last!
A telephone was new fangled!
The letter was all in vogue!
But now we've got our mobiles,
Emails and texts wouldn't you know!
We huddled around the telly!
Black and white for the Coronation!
But now we have got Cable and BskyB,
And countless obscure stations!
We bought our food one day at a time!
But now it's the monthly shop!
With the advent of fridges and freezers,
We shop until we drop!
And then there are all the fiddly things,
That the adverts say we need!
From Cameras Ipods and Memory sticks,
To Playstation and Nintendo Wii!
Do we really need them?
They're indispensable to some!
But if most of the things, we did without,
Then I think we'd have more fun!

57

The Digital Convert

The time is fast approaching

When the telly will go off

There won't be anything left to see

Not even the receding dot

So what am I to do now?

With my screen completely blank

I suppose I'll have to get

What the others have

When I raid my piggy bank

It's time for me to go digital

To upgrade my TV

To get a little set-top box

Or join satellite city

Where dishes cling to every house

Pointing to the sky

Waiting for the Astra satellite

To orbit from on high

I've put off till the bitter end

But I knew the day would come

When I'd be going digital

All around my home

Ten weeks have passed

Now I have a host of gadgetry

From cameras and computers to

Sky, Ipods and DAB

I don't not how I did get by

Without these bits and bobs

It's clever how each gadget works

It saves me lots of jobs

Foreigners

Individuals doing their thing
        Travelling life's course
Through what their day brings
        Helter-skelter to and fro
Rushing around, as if
        There's no tomorrow!
As we pass by, in a moment of time
        Hearing snatched conversation,
As strangers pass by,
        Make you feel that you are a spy!
Eavesdropping sightseers,
        Gazing in wonder!
At things you've long since,
        Stopped to ponder!
Chattering foreigners,
        Cameras in hand!
Newcomers to your
        So common land!
Then comes the day,
        You venture afar!
Then it's your turn to
        Stop and stare!
In someone else's own hometown,
        Just like them,
You'll puzzle and frown!
        With camera in hand,
Whilst your skin turns
        Bright red, on its way
To dark brown!

The Rose

Floribunda Hybrid T
　　　Climbing, Patio
Shrub variety
　　　Each one has its' unique smell
The capacity to make one dwell
　　　When a rose is presented
To your Belle
　　　Its aromatic scent
Makes the heart swell
　　　In love there is nothing
Quite like the rose
　　　To say I love you
Without words
　　　From a Beau

61

Christmas Toys

I heard a noise up in the loft
I climbed up for to see
It came from all the Christmas toys
That adorns my Christmas tree
The time is fast approaching
They sense the mood as well
When they will be let loose again
In the living room for to dwell
Multi-coloured baubles
Bright flashing fairy lights
I can hear them sing and warble
As they get quite uptight
Let us out I hear them cry
As the ladder I ascend
Then descending with said trinkets
Enough to make the Christmas tree bend
Hurry up I hear them cry
It's my turn next they say
As one by one they make their splash
Of colour for Christmas day
They breathe a sigh and grin
They are all awaiting!
Santa and his sleigh

They begin to dance and sway
They fill the home with merriment
Singing cheery songs and ringing bells
Pleased to be free once again
Awaiting Christmas morn
Singing songs of the Christ child
To pave the way for Christmas day
To see the children smile and play
As presents are given and received
The pleasure is there for all to see
As presents they are unwrapped
What is there here for me?
Christmas day it comes and goes
So soon the year it turns
The Christmas toys know time is short
Till in their box they are returned
All sealed up for another year
They go into hibernation
Till Christmas time comes around again
When we will hear once more
All their narration

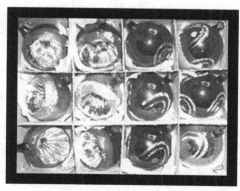

Santa Came Again In April

Santa came again in April

    Because of all the snow

The elves they tried to stop him

    But he made the reindeers go

Confusion reigned in Santa's mind

    When the snow it would not stop

So the spell was nearly broken

    When down chimneys he did drop

He looked around for Christmas trees

    But not one could he find

So he returned his presents to his sleigh

    And left the world behind

Now Ma and Pa can breathe again

    The secret's still intact

Just for one awful moment

    There was a snowy Santa and his sack

What If

What If the sun refused to shine
    The plants they didn't grow
What If the rains they didn't fall?
    The streams they didn't flow
What If my friend we'd never met
    We neither got to know
What If our love, like all the seeds
    We were not allowed to sow
What If the world was dull and drab
    Sombre, cold and grey
What If, but no, I am so sad
    While you are far away
Come home soon my dearest friend
    My love, my soul, my life
What If we make a brand new start?
    My Friend, My love My Wife!

Moody Blue

Isn't life strange is the question that I pose?

As I wander like a gypsy down eternity road.

As I find new horizons I think of you and me

Lost in a lost world, like driftwood all at sea

I know you're out there somewhere

I hear your voice it's it the sky

It's a legend in the mind of this melancholy man

After you came I started talking out of turn

I saw visions of paradise with the eyes of a child

As I beheld the candle of life and the story in your eyes

One step into the light and I had to fall in love

You're my Gemini dream, I'm you're other half in life

Once is enough, I'll be level with you

It's cold outside of your heart

I just don't care it may be a fire

But I'll suffer the slings and arrows

Say it with love, when you lean on me tonight

Our Fates Entwined

In my heart I imagine

A time and a place that we

Could break down any barrier

Pictures for to see

Pray that all our exploits

Will be more than fantasy

Drive away your nightmares

Call attention to what will be

Our fates entwined forever

To live always as one

Being true to one another

Till our time is done

First Love

There's a small place in my heart
For my first love!
You where lost to me
When we were young
And yet
My feelings are as strong
As on that day when we first met
You're the one
I'll never forget
My first love
With your love for life
Your infectious smile
Your cheeky grin
Your deep blue eyes
Your pure, pale skin
Your golden hair
Made my heart melt
Whenever you were near,
If only things had turned out right
But the diagnosis meant you had a fight
At so young an age
Try as you might

You were never meant to win
Fate can be so very cruel
But you'd flash that cheeky grin
You pushed me away
It hurt at the time
Now I know it was for the best
You didn't want me
To share in your test
As I write these words I know
If you were with me now
The outcome may have not been the same
But I know one thing that will never change
Within my heart still burns your flame
So rest in peace my dear first love
Please know I bear no ill will
Always know my first love
I loved you then, I love you now
I know I always will!

Unconditional Love

The one thing that is certain, between man and his dog,

Is the everlasting, unconditional love!

He'll take your moods,

Your tantrums and still,

Love you unconditionally,

Wagging his tail!

He knows what you are thinking,

Before you do yourself!

He'll look up expectantly,

Then he'll give a yelp!

Then it's out for a walk,

He knows it's time,

He's out of the door,

Before the clock chimes!

He'll take all you give,

Good, bad and the like,

He'll love you unconditionally,

For all of his life!

To Love Someone
(Sonnet)

To love someone, to truly care
To worship every lock of hair
To see those eyes and pure skin,
    feel deep emotions stir within
To have, to hold, love and embrace,
    feel your respect will not be misplaced
To feel the joy you have with each other
To be as one, now you're are lovers
To be loyal to each other, whatever life's travails
To be as flowers in full bloom,
    as your love prevails
To see the rising sun on each beautiful day
To let Valentine and Cupid have their way
To allow them both to have their say
To live life to the full, come what may
To let romance blossom from now to ever after
To love now and always your lives
    filled with laughter

Love At First Sight

(Serpentine)

I loved you the first day we met,
        the first day we met you and I
Across a crowded room you I did espy;
        you caught my eye, the crowded room across
We made small talk, danced, then drank wondering each what
        small thoughts about we
Time it went by we then said goodbye,
        we said goodbye till next time
Two days went by till we met again,
        till we met again we two
I love you still, I always will, do you love as much of I
If so, then lets have a whirlwind romance much like our dance,
        say what if
We two settle down, do I see a frown,
        please can we
I would love you to marry me for all eternity
        in wedded bliss you and I
Was that a yes then, I'm not good at guessing,
        please stop you're messing, yes it was
To have and to hold until we are old, until death do we part
        and part we have to
You I'll love to the end, forever a friend,
        I know now I'll always love you!

Fateful Forecast

I stroll along the waters edge,
Beside the stormy sea!
As Neptune, aye and Davy Jones,
Ride white horses filled with glee!
On the lookout for unsuspecting,
Tankers, trawlers and yachts!
And not least, weekend fishermen!
Who get into a spot?
Of bother, there'll be plenty!
As long as the sea is rough,
When the most seasoned of campaigners,
Can be swallowed by a trough!
As waves, they grow much higher!
As Boats, they bob and slew!
God help the men who are unprepared,
The captain and the crew!
Perhaps they will be lucky,
They'll escape the jaws of death!
Perhaps the wind and rain will pass,
But it's safer not to guess!
If the forecast is for storm force winds,
Little ships should stay in port!
Remember all your loved ones,
Davy Jones might break their hearts!

Objet D'art

The musty smell of artefacts

       Are enough to make me swoon?

This scent is always present

       In an auction room

Looking at the furniture

       Made from oak and ash and teak

The china dolls, what tales they'd tell

       If only they could speak

So many lives here intertwined

       Of folk we'll never know

Is this the way my prized possessions

       Will one day be on show?

Contact

Across the universe,

    Many miles away.

Someone is doing the same as me,

    Are you there?

He seems to say!

    Am I the only one like me?

Is my breed unique to here?

    Are there anymore on other worlds?

Say, on that bright star up there!

    I'd like to talk, indeed converse!

If possible over the universe!

    Send messages by radio, and get some back!

Make contact with like –minded souls,

    As an interstellar hack!

Perhaps one day we may even meet,

    Our off –world friends in their Starfleet!

Tempus Fugit

One more year…One more year to go

One more year… To the big Five-O

Forty-nine years… Have come and gone

It seems only yesterday…When I was one

Tempus Fugit…Nay time flies

Seems to me it's gone…In the blink of an eye

What's in store?.. This coming year

Apart from more…Greying of my hair

Time will tell...As the saying goes

I guess I'll just go…With the flow

Take each day…As it turns out

Trying not…To scream and shout

And when at last…Another year is through

I'll find I've still got…Things to do

To accomplish all…I set myself

May take…A little longer

Than it did just…A year ago

When I…Was that much younger!

Torne Di Surrento

Come back Sorrento calls to me
From Naples bay in Italy
What finer place is there to be?
Than with the summer sun on your back
And your hair flowing free

To visit Pompeii
With it's volcanic ruins and rubble
While nearby Vesuvius quietly bubbles
Waiting its turn to cause more trouble

Go to Positano with its caverns and caves
To Salerno with its wartime graves
To Amalfi with its beautiful church and piazza
Evening drinks in Sorrento thereafter

Take a boat to Capri
Or a trip to Rome
It won't be long
Before you're on your way home

Go for a swim
Do the butterfly
Or just relax
And let the day go by

Read a book and forget yourself
It will soon be time to go
When there will be a whisper on the wind
Saying Torne Di Surrento

Brother Mason's Harmony

Brother Junior Warden comes the request!

Could you please supply harmony from one of your guests?

I can supply harmony the brother replies!

Brother mason will you please arise?

As the timid brother takes to the floor,

He wonders what, he's let himself in for!

Should he crack a joke, recite a poem:

Give a monologue or sing a song?

An expectant audience awaits his decision!

He hopes to come through without any derision!

He takes deep breaths and so begins,

His debut performance on his pins!

A joke to start to settle the nerves,

And then a song that's filled with verve!

Another joke then a monologue,

His audience is quite agog!

A final joke then a final song,

As the performance starts to bounce along!

Too soon it seems to come to an end!

As he takes his bow and returns to his friends!

Thanks are given and received,

Once our brother has taken his leave!

I'm pleased that's over and has come to an end!

Not yet it's not, you're on the circuit my friend!

Lest We Forget

What a day to be twenty-one,
     A clear blue sky,
A brilliant sun,
     A contradiction!
There is no birdsong,
     The silence is eerie!
A feeling of unease,
     Fills my being!
As I look at
     Foundations laid out,
Like graves.
     I have visions of grief!
Panic and fear, of
     People I've never met but,
Will not forget!
     The rows of reminders,
Indeed the gas chambers,
     It's painful to the eye!
A pair of huts is full
     Of the inmates memorial!
A tangled, metalled mass,
     A sculpture of a brutal past!

Remember Them

It is an August day,
>I will never forget!
No where, no way, no how,
>I'll never forget the day,
Of my visit to Dachau!
>The torment they went through,
I can't begin to know!
>But I can honestly say,
My heart is filled with sorrow!
>We all know where we were,
The day that Elvis died,
>Likewise J. F. K!
But the day that's most imprinted,
>On my soul,
Is that day in Dachau,
>When I was twenty-one years old.

Lark Ascending

Lark ascending upon high
  I hear your gentle trill
In a clear blue sky
  Hovering so far above
So motionless, so still
  Gliding gently sideways
Calling out your tune
  Majestically outpouring
Your sweet song
  As you keep on soaring
Looking down on all earths creatures
  The surrounding land and all of its features
Waiting your time
  Way up on high
Watching earth's children
  Until the all clear draws nigh
Then when you decide the time is right
  You drop like a stone
Stop in mid-flight
  Check and hover once again
Drop some more
  Hover and soar
Drop again when all is well
  Land below my line of sight
Walk to your nest that you watched in flight
  No better sight is there to see
Than a lark ascending
  Just above me

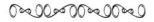

Time

Time is so precious it should not go to waste
  This day could see your last daybreak
It could also see the last breath you take
  It's good to feel the air on your skin
To waste your time is such a sin
  Make something happen it won't come to you
It's so easy just to sit and stew
  Live each day, fill it with joy
Anger is folly, don't destroy
  Today's the first day of the rest of your life
So keep friendships close and love your wife
  Never go to bed in a fit of rage
Say sorry, you may never turn the page
  Time is so precious
It should not go to waste
  As this may be your last daybreak

Time and Tide

Crashing rolling weaving curling
 Like fingers outstretching
Massaging the shore
 Marching retreating
Forever beating
 Relentless cascades
Upwardly dangerous
 Pounding and spraying
Rocks turn to stones
 Through eons of breaking
Stealthy, mesmeric
 Ever onward
Ocean currents
 Tirelessly
Ebb and flow
 Beating time
To creations music
 As mankind
Their daily lives
 Come and go

Balancing Books

Balancing books
     Three at a time
Holding their threads
     In my head and
My mind
     Their topics and themes
Their storylines varied
     Holding them in my mind
Keeps me mentally
     Aware and
Giving my brain
     A good workout; keeping
Alzheimer's at bay
     Is my way of
Coping with life
     From day to day
I know that
     Some find it hard
To read even one
     But I find balancing books
With my mind
     Is great fun!

The Dear Departed

I've met some characters
    In my time
At work and play
    They were all just fine
Some had their foibles
    But then
Don't we all
    Some turned a trick
Would love to see a fall
    But most of all
My colleagues of old
    Were very sound
Or so I'm told
    Some would laugh
Some would joke
    The odd ones
They were queer folk
    I loved them all
Respected them too
    But now I find
There are just a few
    Of my work colleagues left
From the day
    That I started
As many are now
    The dear departed
Gone to meet
    The Lord above
Though sadly missed
    They'll be dearly loved

Sir Bobby

Sleep well Sir Bobby
    It's been good to know you
Not personally
    Though
It felt that way to me
    You will be missed
By one and all
    Of the hearts you touched
Not just in football
    A true Geordie Gent
With a heart of gold
    You left an Impression
On the young and the old
    So rest in peace
You fought a good fight
    Till we meet again
I'll just say
    Goodnight

The Angel

There's a chunk of metal by the motorway

That people gaze at day after day

It's the biggest waste of space I say

Could someone please take it away

The Angel of The North came down

Ten years ago and I still frown

In all that time it hasn't grown

On me each time I go to town

It looks like rust, a shade of brown

An eyesore to behold I groan

Will some please just tear it down?

It's had its time I moan

I'm sure some people like it

Think it's a joy to see

But how often do they view it

I see it regularly

And it does

Absolutely nothing for me

Then again it inspired

This poetry

The Bridges Of Tyne

There are many fine bridges
       Throughout the country
But the bridges of Tyne
       Look the finest to me
From the Redheugh *(Reg Huff)*
       To the Millenium Eye
They look splendid
       Set against the morning sky
When the blinking eye, at sunset
       Looks west at the rest
They sparkle like gems
       Neatly set
A better sight
       I've yet to see
Than that river of light
       Flowing out to sea
Silhouetted against
       A red gold sky
So very pleasing
       To the eye

Poetic musings

We're lucky to have

    Seven bridges so fine

Between Newcastle and Gateshead

    Spanning the old river Tyne

What a welcome sight

    When returning home

Those multi-coloured bridges

    Are the best sights bar none!

The Hug

I sit on the sofa, holding a mug
       Then there's a nose under my elbow
Of the dog that I love
       He pleads with sad eyes
As he snuggles in tight
       So I give him a hug and
Settle in for the night
       My heart rate slows down
As I stroke his coat
       Then I hear a deep sigh
Coming from his throat
       At peace with ourselves
As night it draws nigh
       Then his head it rests, on my thigh
In for the duration,
       However long that may be
Settled, comfortably enjoying
       Each other's company!

Playing With Numbers

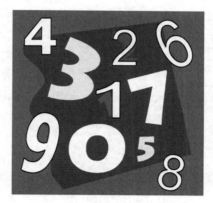

Playing with numbers
One to nine
All jumbled up
To bend the mind

Some easier than others
Tricky ones all
One false move
And the game will stall

Number crunching
Is quite addictive
But to finish one
Fiendishly set
It is amazing,
The satisfaction one gets

The Interview

Welcome to the interview

    Please put yourself at your ease

Our questions aren't meant to stump you

    They are just a bit of a tease

There's coffee, tea or water

    Please help yourself throughout

I hope we don't intimidate

    If we do please don't walk out

I'd like to start by asking

    Do you know what the job entails?

You should as you applied for

    The job and all its pitfalls

Next I'd like to ask you

    Who you think you're working for

Is that right, you think

    The company is worth a whole lot more

I'd like you now to present your work

    You've put together overnight

Please don't be shy, project yourself

    Let your ideas take flight

That was quite enjoyable

  We understood it and

Are impressed

  The edges I know need sharpening

No doubt it will be better when

  This has been addressed

The questions come one after another

  One about this and yes about t'other

When will it end I ask myself

  As a question I once more fend

Then I realise to my relief

  Were almost at the end

Just one more thing before you go

  What would you do on your first day?

A prudent answer is then returned

  Now I hope and pray.

Footprints

Silently floating
Spiralling drifting
Ever downward
To the ground
Lying softly
Crisp and even
Virgin white
Till footsteps pound
Laying hitherto
Unknown trails
To all points of the compass
Till the next snowfalls
Deeper still
Footprints disappearing
As winters chill
Take hold in the clearing

Night Terrors

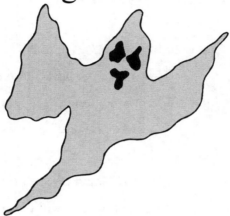

Vampires, Werewolves,
    Ghouls and Ghosts
Things that go bump in the night
    Shades and Wraiths and
Poltergeists,
    Always good for a fright
Shivering, withering,
    Nervous, on edge
Confronting a lifetime of fears
    Till the purple predawn twilight
Breaks the dawn of a
    Brand new day

Wasps

Do I not like wasps?

    They make me shiver and shake

I get chilled to the bone

    When sweat starts to break

I go all pale

    As beads stand on my brow

Will someone come and kill that wasp

    Please will they please do it now?

To hear the buzz of an angry wasp

    It just makes my skin crawl

I really don't like wasps at all

    They look bad enough on rugby shirts

Where I know they cannot harm me

    But to see just one wasp

Real and alive

    Well I'm afraid

I go quite barmy!

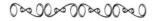

Summer Time (Acrostic)

Summer is here

Under clear blue skies

Mowers mow lawns now the grass is dry

Men and woman walk hand in hand

Everyone enjoying the summer sun

Relaxing in the balmy breeze, leaning up against the barks of trees

Taking doggies for a walk or just sitting on blankets having a talk

Ideal weather to stop and stare share a moment without a care

Many people, animals and birds, go about their day as if in herds, till

Evening comes with fall of night, tomorrow comes they all take flight

Walk An Autumn Day

To walk about in

Clear autumn

Weather, Enjoying the sight of all

The trees decked out in all their finery, Many

Different colours on show as the autumn winds begin

To blow, Shaking and ruffling the leaves as they turn too many

Colours of beauty so warm, the shortest of seasons so pretty and yet

I love this time of year

So fresh, so crisp, so pure, so sweet and so pleasing to the eye, as the

sunlight it flashes through the trees

Out of a clear blue sky, an autumn walks a pleasure with every

single stride,

A carpet of leaves underneath my feet makes soft rustle

As I go, walking through woodland without a care

As the autumn breeze blows through my hair,

The mist rolling in as the day it

Is nearly done

It is time to go

Autumn Starlight

When Orion the hunter
      Fights Taurus the prey
When Castor and Pollux
      Come out to play
With Sirius the dog
      On cold frosty nights
I know that autumn is here now
      As summer takes flight
Followed by misty mornings
      With leaves of all shades
A multicoloured patchwork
      Throughout woodland glades
Gold's, browns and reds
      With some evergreens
A more beautiful sight
      Will never be seen
A carpet of leaves beneath my feet
      Rustle and stir as I walk alongside
A cool woodland stream
      The water reflecting the sun through the trees
Cool air on my face from the autumn breeze
      Wrapped up warm with extra layers
I can still enjoy autumn and all its crisp days

A Walk In Autumn

I love to
Walk in the woods
In autumn weather
Enjoying the sight of all the trees
Decked out in all their finery,
Many different colours on show
As the autumn winds begin to blow,
Shaking and ruffling the leaves as they turn
To many colours of beauty so warm,
The shortest of seasons so pretty and yet
I love this time of year
So fresh, so crisp, so pure, so pleasing to the eye
An autumn walk is always a pleasure with every single stride
A carpet of leaves underneath my feet
Make a soft rustle as I go
Walking through woodland with the one I love
Without a thought or care
Taking in the wondrous sights
As the autumn breeze blows through my hair
The mist rolling in as the day it wears on
I wonder where the time it has gone
Now I know It's time to go

Autumn Gold

(Acrostic)

All

Undergrowth is turning gold and multicoloured shades
        in between it seems to me
Trees also burnished with multiple hues make the woodland
        a variegated sea
Under bright blue skies I hear cries as geese in formation fly
        south in their winter Vee
Marvellous, scenic, picturesque landscapes of

Never ending beauty doth the eye behold and see

Glorious gatherings

Of colours abound greens reds gold orange and brown

Least of all seasons short but so sweet

Done too soon

Harvest Moon

The silvery rays
    Of the harvest moon
Bring autumn chills
    Where temperatures soon
Drop by degrees
    From their summer highs
When the weather was warm
    With sun high in the sky
But soon the equinox will arrive
    The sun will then sink
Low in the sky
    Winds will blow
Leaves will fall
    As autumns golden period stalls
So we gather our crops
    For all too soon
There'll be a waning of
    The harvest moon

Harvest Time

The time of year has come again
To pick the apples, collect the grain
Harvesting corn from morning till night
Baling hay with all our might
Gathering crops tilling the land
Sowing the seed for the future
And
Giving praise to the good lord above
For the harvested food for the ones that we love

Autumn leaf

One descending leaf
In midair suspended hangs
In a spiders web

105

Old Year Remembered

Another year is nearly gone

Most eventful

Especially for some

Times of joy

Times of sorrow

What will next year offer

We'll find out on the morrow

To find out that we'll have to wait

For no one knows what is his or her fate

Happy New Years

My Favourite State

My favourite State is

Organised chaos

As I know where everything goes

To go into a room

That has just been done

Puts me in a spin

Why can't things just

Be left alone

Could the duster not

Just skirt around

It will be time to

Hoover and dust again

Before everything misplaced

Has once again been found

Story Lines

The story was in the telling
    A hidden meaning dwelling
But it was right there to my surprise
    When once found I realised
The truth that lies between fact and fiction
    Was the way we depict and
Relate a yarn we hear from relations
    Passed down the ages
By husbands, wives, sisters and brothers
    To generations yet to come
Of times past and how it was fun
    To live in times of yesteryear
Living life without a care
    Then things change
As trouble brews
    Problems come in not ones
But twos
    Conflicts abound problems need sorting
But life's tapestry is such
    As to be ongoing
The story is in the telling
    The hidden meanings are dwelling
But all will come right in the end
    If you can tell your foe from friend

Romancing (Nonet)

Romancing the sweetheart you love

Courting with flowers and notes

With affectionate cards

Or a single red rose

On bended knee show

Eternal love

To your love

From her

Beau

(Acrostic)

Romantic evening by candlelight

Over a table hands held tight

Making eye contact excluding all others

Announcing to the world here are two lovers

Nights like these are so precious, so few

Courtships of true lovers are such a heady brew

Igniting passions so deep in the heart

Never intending each other to part

Glorious Saint Valentine was there from the start

My Snowman Sentry

The beauty of a winter's day

As children in the snow, they play

Throwing snowballs, sledging hills

Making snowmen, and all it entails

Coal for eyes and for teeth

With a carrot for the nose and

A scarf underneath

Made to last the span of time

That winters grip holds

That sentry of mine

His lifespan relies

On the cold winters chill

Because when the sun shines and

The snow starts to thaw

My snowman sentry will,

Be no more!

The Inglorious Twelfth

Does anybody tell the grouse?
      Today is August the twelfth
The day that's known as glorious
      When beaters approach with stealth
All he does is sit there his business trying to mind
      When those crafty little beaters creep up from behind
A whoosh and a thwack as heather cracks
      He's shocked into action
Up he flies into the skies
      Then he hears a gun and changes direction
A sweeping arc and then a spark
      As shot is upward rising
Too soon the grouse can do no more
      As the shooter bags a prize one
So it goes till December tenth
      When they head count the survivors
Until next year on August twelfth
      The moorland grouse can thrive

Christmas

Christmas is the time of year

    To wish your fellow man good cheer

A time to remember the Christ child

    Gentle Jesus meek and mild

Who received gold frankincense and myrrh?

    Grew up to carry the whole worlds cares

So please remember at Christmas time

    The legacy he left behind

Be kind and forgive your fellow man

    Receive your gifts as best you can

Running
(Anaphora)

Running ones' life can be complicated
Running a home needs dedication
Running for office raising ones' station
Running for President of the whole nation
Running flat out for a lap or a mile
Running a group to make people smile
Running around on the go all the time
Running on empty but feeling just fine
Running a temperature, feeling unwell
Running through purple heather over a fell
Running for charity, having a laugh
Running hot water, filling a bath
Running a book, taking a bet
Running from the law, they haven't caught me yet
Running the job getting things done
Running on time, like clockwork, such fun
Running quite late, being short of time
Running for the bus I hope I catch mine
Running for cover in inclement weather
Running a service for the public to wherever
Running the shower at the end of the day
Running the rule over thoughts that held sway
Running is over, tonight's time for rest
Running will start once more on the morrow
      I hope I'm at my best!

Give Thanks
(Anaphora)

Give thanks each day that you wake up
Give thanks for the friends you make
Give thanks that you have a good life
Give thanks for the love that you share
Give thanks that you have one another
Give thanks for the food provided
Give thanks for the air you breathe
Give thanks for the birds, bees and trees
Give thanks for the freedom to vote
Give thanks but please take note
Give thanks you weren't born oppressed
Give thanks you have been born blessed
Give thanks for the lush green country
Give thanks for the golden sand and the deep blue sea
Give thanks that the good lord decided
Give thanks that he sent you, me
Give thanks for our love for each other
Give thanks for our sisters and brothers
Give thanks for our fathers and mothers
Give thanks for the time we have left
Give thanks that we've both done our best
Give thanks for all the right decisions you make
Give thanks for the times you get a break
Give thanks to the good lord above
Give thanks he filled our hearts with love

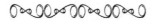

If Only I Could See My Way

If only
I could see my way
Get around from day to day

Take what comes at me,
Come what may

Let fate's hand deal
And have its' say

Take it on the chin
And still not sway

Perhaps
I'll get to break away

From the ties that bind
And let me pay
The ferryman

So I can play
In another land
Far, far away

If only
I could see my way

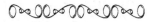

I Always Get away With It

I said I could do it!
Though I nearly blew it!
There was nothing to it
If they only knew it!
At the start of the day,
 That led up to it!

It was only a prank!
I've got away with it,
I think?
No one followed!
As I deeply swallowed!
And now I'll have that drink!

I always get away with it!
Because I'm such a clever wit!
I play my cards close to my chest!
Then I can outwit the very best!

Some may say I cheat!
And jump to their feet!,
But I do it so well,
They never can tell!
As I slip a card!
They might try very hard,
But my magic tricks are so neat!

116

Step Into Spring

Dew on the grass
        It's spring at last
The misty morn'
        The frost all but gone
Sunlight shining through the trees
        As winter is finally brought to its knees
A light wind blows fresh from the west
        Birds in full song puff out their breasts
Chirping whistling, heralding
        The start of a brand new day,
Crocus, daffodils and tulips
        Begin to nod and sway
A brand new season
        In a brand new year
Watch the children run and play
        As snow is all but confined to the past
Clinging to hedgerows as we walk past
        Soon it will be gone for good
As the days draw long
        As trees come into bud
What better place is there to be?
        Than to step into spring
            Just you and me!

Valentine

(Nonet)

Valentine as king of all love hearts
Do take a message please for me
Tell my true love adore her
Love her eternally
Hear me King of love
My hands and eyes
They plead
To love
She

Acrostic

Virile lover of women and girls
Any sight of you puts their heads in a whirl
Lover sublime with a tongue of silver
Enraptured girls all a quiver
Not one disappointed by your advances
Taken in one and all as you leave them in trances
Impassioned lover of life, love and laughter
New conquests to be made
Endless passion thereafter

Daffodils

A carpet
Of bright yellow
Heads nodding
To and fro in the breeze
They never make a sound
In trumpeting their calls
In the meadow
On the wind

Norman

My wife came across Norman

In Two thousand and six

A Norfolk Canary

Who was in a fix?

Let go from an Aviary

With one deformed claw

Mistaken for a sparrow

By a civil servant who saw

Him flapping his wings

Outside of the window

Looking for help

So off Sheila did go

A phone call was made

I picked up and received

A Norfolk I called Norman

Plucky for his breed

Five years on he's still going strong

Tapping and flapping and singing his song

With Co-Co for company

His Cockatiel mate

We were pleased we rescued Norman

Before it was too late!

Acrostic Almanac

JANUARY

Joyous celebrations herald in the brand new year
Auld Lang synes' kindness, we'll drink a cup of my dear
New Year resolutions how long will they hold firm
Until first sign of weakness, just as in yesteryear
Anniversaries and birthdays come around again
Rain and sleet and hale and snow all seasons rolled into one
Yet January at the new years dawn can bring so much fun

FEBRUARY

Fingers frozen to the bone
Ever deeper is the winter
But birds start singing in the trees
Robins, Chaffinches and Linnets their songs carry on the breeze
Unwary people get caught out on thin ice
Arm in arm and hand in hand couples venture out for a tryst
Romances start to bloom again as days they get much longer
Yes I will is heard on the fourteenth as Valentines influence
    becomes much stronger

MARCH

Misty mornings as days stretch out
All around trees and flowers bloom
Raising hopes of a flaming June
Cuckoos herald in the first day of spring
Hurricane winds say think again

APRIL

Arriving birds fly in from the south
Purple heather is all about
Rain and showers are par for the course
Ideal conditions for sap to rise
Lifting our spirits as they beautify

MAY

Month of weddings
All decked out in finery
Young couples tie the knot for a lifetime, we'll see?

JUNE

June arrives as temperatures rise
Under clear blue cloudless skies
Not always the case I know
Enjoying each day like there's no tomorrow

JULY

Joyous times arrive at last
Under blazing sun take holidays and rest
Lazing about or wearing your best
Youthful exuberance putting parents to the test

AUGUST

Autumn colours soon will arrive
Under shorter days and cloudier skies
Great Helios rises up still bright
Until the day draws to an end but we still have balmy nights
Shooters of grouse arrive on the twelfth
Taking all they can bag then come back again

SEPTEMBER

Splendid colours begin to show
Evenings draw further in as autumn winds blow
People enjoy the last days of summer
Taking the air arm in arm with one another
England in autumn is a beauty to behold
Marked by many colours from brown through to gold
Blooms at their best in garden shows
Every type of vegetable grown by those who know how
Rigorously checked winners take a bow

OCTOBER

Oh for the days to be longer than this
Combines in the fields are hard to miss
Threshing the corn the wheat and the barley
On into the night with lights burning brightly
Balers come next trying to outpace the rain
Expressly parcelled and loaded for barn
Remember the clocks, they fall back again

NOVEMBER

Nights are drawing darker still
Ominous signs of winters chill
Vanquished autumn short but sweet
Every-ones at the party on bonfire night
Marvel at the fireworks as they cascade through the sky
Brilliant showers of myriad sparklers up on high
Evergreens stand amongst leafless trees
Rocking and swaying on the strengthening breeze

DECEMBER

Darkest of months arrives at last
Eerily calm before the cold winter blast
Christmas cheer to lift spirits high
Erasing the gloom at least for a time
Marking the birth of Christ our lord
Bearer of the sins of the world
Ending the year as we began
Ringing in the New Year, to begin again!

Random Thoughts

Some times my thoughts are random
When the muse strikes me
My pen nib it starts twitching
As my ideas they enthuse
Writing away on paper
The random thoughts my brain devises
Page after page of material
Some good, some bad, some average
So many moods enfold me
So much to see and dwell
So many different topics
Situations for to tell
Tales they are a plenty
In many styles and voices
Subjects are so varied
So many different choices
Then something leaps straight at me
For now I am decided
On the story or poem to be composed
I set to work with my head down
With my attention undivided

Civic Pride

Do the locals care any more?

Do they have civic pride?

It sometimes makes me wonder

What lies behind their eyes?

Broken glass and litter

Cans and bottles strewn around

The council workers doing constant battle

So that we might see the ground

Some day the offenders may realise the folly of their ways

But I'm sure there will be someone else to make the mess anew

There'll always be a struggle with a certain generation

To instill in them the civic pride and selfless dedication

We can but hope the time will come

When their behaviour improves beyond measure

Then we can all share in our civic pride

While getting around will be a pleasure

In The Chair

Many masons have come
Have been and gone
Have sat in the chair of King Solomon
Ruling the lodge gavel in hand
Doing the very best that they can
Working the ritual in various degrees
Bringing their candidates to their knees
Some are naturals at what they do
Others have problems getting through
But all have the D. C. as their guiding light
Aware of the brother who try as he might
Struggles through passages oblique and obscure
Where no amount of revision will make him sure
Of the line as presented and laid out on the page
Will sink in the brothers' brain so sage
All's well that ends well when the lodge is close tyled
So till next month, with fresh candidate we will rest for a awhile
The next day comes with a terrible thought
Next month will come soon, so the ritual is sought!

W. Bro George Lark Ellison
Earl Of Durham Lodge No 1274

My Life On The Line

First I was a shunter
At Heaton coach sidings
Happy as a sandman
In times of glad tidings

Everyone enjoyed his work
Though sometimes it was hard
But everyman pulled the same way
It was a very happy yard

It had its' share of characters
Much as we have today
But work was more enjoyable
In every single way

There was still plotting and scheming
At times you turned a hair
But no one stabbed you in the back
There was always time to care

Next I went to Lamesley
To Tyne Marshalling Yard
The reason that I went there
Was to be a freight train guard

The friendliness was in the air
From one day to another
The place was like a holiday camp
Indeed there could be no other

No other place quite like Tyne Yard
Where no one had a care
Where all had a sense of being brothers in arms
While laughter filled the air

Indeed this was my downfall
As I stayed too long at Tyne
As when I went up for promotion
I found the boat had left me behind

For a time I'd worked at Central
Newcastle was not for me
Where they all had serious faces
A sign of things to be

I only lasted twenty months
Then got promoted back to Tyne
To find a charge-mans wages
Devalued in due time

Now ten years on, twenty-three in all
I come full circle back to Heaton
I'm still being paid less than a conductor guard
But I suppose life must go on

I wondered would I ever climb the sweet ladder to success
The answer I know to my cost, I missed the boat whilst enjoying life
So I'm just happy with my lot with forty years fast approaching
With my retirement and leisure time and a lot less strife

My Copyright

Why do I like poetry?

    It has certain symmetry

Laying down thoughts

    Words and deeds

Allowing the pen

    To take the lead

Sometimes you find

    You've written a gem

At other times

    You think ahem

Perhaps next time

    It will come together

When more thought

    Is put into the subject matter

But whatever I write

    Whether good, bad or trite

I know one thing for certain

    It's my copyright!

Thank You!

For taking the time to read

My most inspired poetry,

Until next time we meet

Hear my refrain

Please read these poems

Again and again!

George L. Ellison

Poetic musings

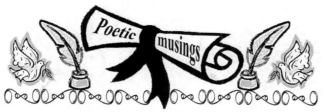

A.P.F.P.Anthology Book

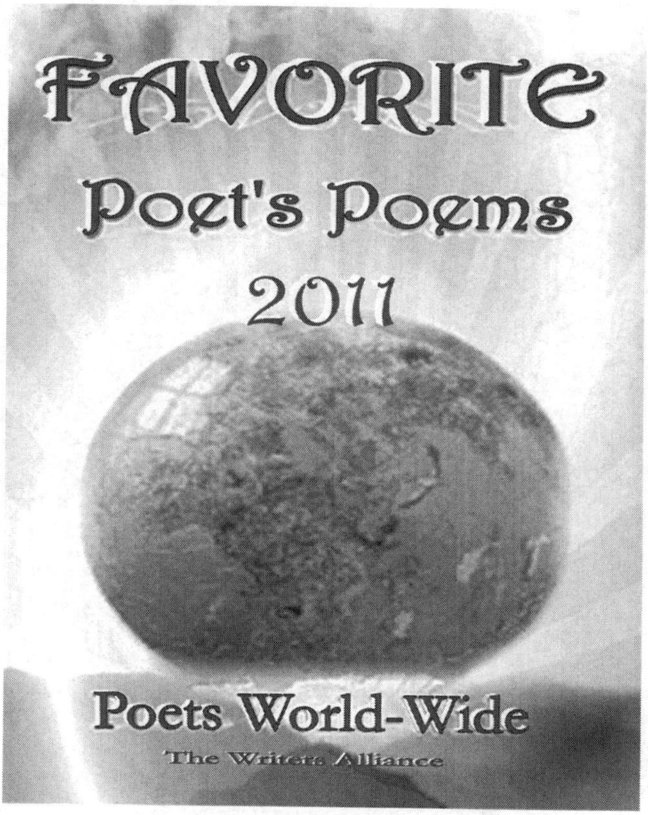

Featuring George and many of today's
Best loved Poets

http://stores.lulu.com/store.php?fAcctID=620220

Other A.P.F.P.Books Featuring George

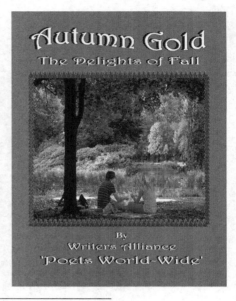

The Spring Season Book Soon To Follow

A.P.F.P. Authors / Book Titles

Patricia Ann Farnsworth-Simpson:
Styles Aplenty Miles Galore: Windows of Light:
Life's Carousel: A Bundle of Muse: The Twinkles:
Flick The Karate Pig: Jack the Lad:
The Wizard the Witch and Joe the Toe:
A Compilation of Tales to Thrill and Chill:
Stories To Thrill and Delight: A Deathly Obsession:
The Rats & The Cats: Mogullygee And Me:

Carolyn Sconzo   My Garden is Growing:

Christina R Jussaume   Amazing Pets & Animals:
Joseph's Star of Eternal Promise:
Spiritual Living Waters: To God Give The Glory:
Spiritual Enlightenment: Spiritual Encouragement

Dee   Timeless Romance

Dena M Ferrari   Poetry From The Hearth

Erich J Goller   Trojan Horse: Groovy:
My Candle Kept on Burning:

Jacquelyn Sturge
Live, Love Laugh A Lot:
Live, Love Laugh With Me Through Poetry A to Z

J. Elwood Davis   The Blue Collar Scholar:

Jennifer Lee Wilson   Fantasy and Foibles

Joanne Agee   Born To Be A Rebel:

Joe Hartman   Pieces of Existence:

John Henson   Shadow Dancer: Broken Wings:

Joree Williams   Ariella: Living With Cancer:

Karen O'Leary   Whispers

Kathleen Charnes-Zvetkoff
Embroidered Limericks: Embroidered Poetry:

Kathleen Edminson   Kath's Choices:

Lynne M. Cullen   The Orange Flame Within

Lou Lenhart   Life is a Gift Everlasting To Treasure:

MAFLongfellow   American Pie Poetry:

Mary Ann Duhart   From Out of The Pit I Cried:
Duhart Expressions   Writing With Styles:

Michael L Schuh   The Fruit of my Pen: But Its Mine:
Mike and Joe: :   Spiritual Thoughts on Love and Life:
The Porter Family: The Cross   Mike's Book of Song Lyrics:

Quarter Moon Poet   Sojourners:

A.P.F.P. Authors / Book Titles

Ralph Stott   Legends for Lunch Time

Richard W, Lamp   Ramblings of a Recovery Mind

Richard A Rousay   Choose the Right Walk With Noah:
Choose The Right and Walk With Ruth
Choose The Right Walk with Alma:

Robert Hewett Sr   Thunderfoot:
Down The Road We Came:

Roger L Scott   _Letters from the Hills:
The Last Trail Ride: The Gifts of Pendrall:

Rochelle Fischer   Mystery in The Mist

William Garret & Rochelle Fischer
Rosewood: Poems & Promises:

Anthology Books By Poets World-Wide
Poetic Words To Support The Troops:
Patriot Passionate Poems For 9 /11
The Magic of Michael Jackson: The Lucky Grub:
The Butterbee Book: Precious Prayers:
Standing Tall When Feeling Small:
Practical Poetic Anthology:
Favorite Poets Poems 2008 / 2009 / 2010 / 2011

*All these Authors including more about George can be seen
on their own web- pages at   www.apfpublisher.com

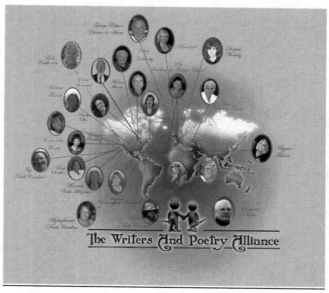

www.patthepoet.com